Anonymous

Taxation of Railroads and Railroad Securities

Anonymous

Taxation of Railroads and Railroad Securities

ISBN/EAN: 9783337415242

Printed in Europe, USA, Canada, Australia, Japan

Cover: Foto ©Suzi / pixelio.de

More available books at **www.hansebooks.com**

TAXATION

OF

Railroads and Railroad Securities.

REPORT OF A COMMITTEE

TO A

CONVENTION OF RAILROAD COMMISSIONERS

Held at Saratoga Springs, June 10, 1879,

TOGETHER WITH A

SUMMARY OF LAWS IN RELATION TO RAILROAD TAXATION IN
FORCE IN THE VARIOUS STATES OF THE UNION
AS WELL AS FOREIGN COUNTRIES.

———◆•◆———

MADISON, WIS.:
DAVID ATWOOD, STATE PRINTER.
1880.

STATE OF WISCONSIN.

IN SENATE.

In the senate on the 23d of January, Senator Woodman offered the following resolution :

Res. No. 16, S.

Resolved, That the railroad commissioner is requested to furnish the senate with the report of the committee of the national convention of railroad commissioners on the subject of the taxation of railroads and railroad securities, together with the abstract of the laws of various states and nations on the same subject, which is ' embodied therewith, and that the clerk of the senate, on receipt of said report, is hereby directed to cause twelve hundred copies thereof to be printed, one thousand of which shall be for the use of the legislature, and the remainder for the official use of the railroad commissioner.

The resolution was laid over, under the rules, and on the 26th was taken up in its order and adopted.

MADISON, *January* 27, 1880.

Hon. J. M. BINGHAM,

    Lt. Governor and President of the Senate:

SIR : I have the honor to transmit herewith for the use of the senate, the inclosed report of committee of railroad commissioners on taxation of railroads and railroad securities made under date of December 1, 1879, with the accompanying compendium of laws of different states and nations on the subject of railroad taxation, in obedience to Res. No. 16, S., and respectfully request that the same be printed.

Very respectfully,

      A. J. TURNER,

      Railroad Commissioner.

REPORT ON TAXATION OF RAILROADS

AND RAILROAD SECURITIES.

The committee appointed at the last (Columbus) convention of railroad commissioners to examine into and report the methods of taxation as respects railroads and railroad securities, now in use in the various states of the Union, as well as in foreign countries, and, further, to report a plan for an equitable and uniform system for such taxation, present the following

REPORT.

Shortly after the last convention of commissioners, your committee issued a circular and accompanying interrogatories in relation to the matter referred to them for investigation, which were sent to all the state executives, and to a large number of the leading railroad corporations of the country. Through the courtesy of the State Department at Washington, the representatives of the national government at the principal capitals in Europe were also called upon for information on the railway tax systems there in use. As a result, some sixty answers were, in all, received, covering the various states of the Union, Canada, England, France, Belgium, Holland, Germany, Russia, Switzerland and Austro-Hungary. The information contained in these answers is much of it of great value, especially in the case of the documents relating to the systems of taxation in use in foreign countries. These the committee have printed in full as part of the present report, as the facts and statements contained in them are not elsewhere to be found in any easily accessible shape. A compendium of the systems in use in all the states of the Union has been prepared, and likewise forms a part of this report.

On examining this compendium of state systems in present use in this country, it will at once be observed that they are much more varied than would naturally be supposed, or, perhaps, than would have been thought possible. Generally, it may be said, there is no one principle running through the various systems de-scribed ; and further, that there is no method of taxation possible to be devised which is not at this time applied to railroad prop-erty in some part of this country. So far as those now well recog-nized principles which should be at the basis of all systems of taxation are concerned, they would as a rule seem to have been utterly ignored.

In two adjoining states, for instance, with roads belonging to one company operating in both, will be found on one side of the line a system, simple, direct, equitable, imposing a moderate and fixed burden from which there is no escape, while on the other side of the line will be met a system which can be said to be based on nothing more reliable than arbitrary guess-work. In' certain states, the railroads are apparently looked upon as a species of wind-fall from which everything which can be exacted in the way of taxation is so much pure gain. In other states they es-cape with very slight and wholly disproportionate burdens. The franchise tax, the gross and net earnings tax, the personal property tax, the realty tax, are all met with indiscriminately ; applied sometimes by local boards, sometimes by boards of state equali-zation, but almost invariably in utter disregard of any principle.

A more striking, and in some respects discouraging, example of general confusion, as regards an important matter of fiscal legis-lation could hardly be imagined.

The conclusion reached by the committee as the result of their investigations can be very briefly stated. The requisites of a cor-rect system of railroad, as of other taxation, are that it should, in so far as it is possible, be simple, fixed, proportionate, easily ascer-tainable and susceptible of ready levy. Very few of the systems now in use in this country were found to possess any of these requisites. So far from being fixed, they are most of them ex-tremely arbitrary and fluctuating. Neither are they proportionate, as in some cases the measure of valuation is the market price of securities ; in others, the arbitrary estimates of appraisers ; in yet others, gross receipts ; and in others, local assessment. That the tax should be almost impossible of ascertainment under these

circumstances does not need to be said. As to being susceptible
of ready levy, any tax assessed on and paid by a railroad corporation is that; but it would appear that a large portion of the
taxes now nominally levied must either be evaded, or else are in
the nature of double taxation, for the securities on which they
are assessed are in the eye of the law personal property, accessible at the residence of the owner.

If, therefore, these securities, whether bonds or stock, are taxed
to the corporation in the state where its road is situate1, they are
as personal property subject to a further tax in the place of the
holder's residence, if he happens to reside in another state; if
such securities are not taxed to the corporations, then, whether
they are taxed at all must depend upon the honesty of the holder
wherever he lives, or the astuteness of the local tax-gatherer.
The utmost inducement to fraud and evasions is thus systematic-
ally held out. For the conscientious holder of stock or bonds
there may be no escape from double taxation of the most oppres-
sive kind, while for the unscrupulous the door for evasion is wide
open.

The conclusion at which your committee arrived was, that all
the requisites of a sound system were found in taxes on real property and on gross receipts, and in no others — in fact, that when
these were properly imposed, no other taxes were or could be
necessary, as nothing would escape untaxed. Under this system,
the real estate of the railroad corporations, held for corporate use
outside of their right of way, would be locally assessed exactly in
the same way as the real estate of private persons or of other corporations adjoining it was assessed. There would be no distinc-
tion made in regard to it. It is the ordinary tax on real property.
Beyond that a certain fixed percentage, established by law and of
general application, should be assessed on the entire gross earnings of the corporations, and this should be in lieu of all forms of
taxation on what is known as personal property. Under this
system the rolling stock of the corporation would not be assessable; nor its securities, whether stock or bonds, either indirectly
through the corporation or directly in the hands of those owning
them. The entire burden, be the same more or less, would be
imposed in one lump on the corporation and levied directly. It

does not need to be pointed out that this system is perfectly simple; that under it taxation is fixed by a general law and not by
local valuations; that it is thoroughly proportionate, inasmuch as
the amount levied depends on the volume of gross receipts ; finally,
it can be ascertained by any one, and can by no possibility be
evaded.

The apportionment of a levy on gross receipts among the several states through which a single railroad may run is in this
country undoubtedly attended with much difficulty, and the committee have given careful consideration to the subject. The conclusion at which they have arrived is that it should be made a
matter of mutual understanding among the states, and that, as the
levies must be independent, they should be apportioned according
to mileage. That is, real estate owned by each corporation, outside of its right of way, should be locally assessed where it is situated, without regard to the fact that it belongs to a corporation
and is used for railroad purposes. The vast and costly terminal
grounds in New York, Chicago and all the other great trade-cen-
tres would thus be locally taxed at those centres, and on the basis
of valuation for similar adjoining land there in use. Real estate
in the country, on the other hand, would be taxed at the country
or agricultural valuation. The realty outside of the right of way
being thus disposed of for purposes of taxation on fixed principles easily understood, the entire gross earnings of the corporations should be subject to assessment by each state through which
its road might run, in the proportion which the miles of the road
in that state bear to its whole number of miles. The percentage
of the levy would then be greater or smaller according to the law
of the state, but the proportion of the whole amount upon which
the levy was to be made would be fixed and always easy of ascertainment.

The disposition to be made of the tax thus levied when paid
into the hands of the state authorities — whether it should be retained in the state treasury or distributed among localities, either
those through which the road might run, or those in which the
holders of its securities reside — would be matter for adjustment
by legislation. It could either be retained in the state treasury or
paid back into the local treasuries of the counties or towns in which

the roads are located on mileage proportions, or ratably distributed among all the municipalities of the state. It is a tax on transportation, whether of persons or property. It is very possibly as equitable a method of raising money by taxation as can be devised. If it could, therefore, once be uniformly and properly adjusted, the distribution of the results of the tax would present very few difficulties. All communities and every part of each community are dependent more or less directly on railroad transportation. A general tax upon it, if properly imposed, would be felt not unequally by all, and might perhaps not unjustly be shared by all. Where the tax on railroads is now levied as an entirety by the state government, the most usual method of distribution is to divide it among the counties and municipalities through which each road runs in proportion to the length of it therein. In Massachusetts the tax is paid over to the place of residence of the individual stockholder, and any undistributed balance is paid into the treasury of the state. In Michigan the whole amount of the tax is paid to and retained by the state, being devoted to special purposes. In Mississippi, where there is a franchise tax, one-half of it goes to the counties through which the road runs, the balance to the state. In New Hampshire, again, one-fourth of the tax is paid to the towns through which the road passes, in proportion to the amount expended in each town for right of way and taxes. The other three-quarters is divided among the towns in proportion to the stock owned therein. In this respect, therefore, as in all others, the existing state systems afford every variety of precedent. The disposition to be made of a tax after it is collected, in no way, however, affects the question of the proper method of collecting it. It must so largely depend on local exigencies that no general rule regulating it would seem to be possible.

Finally, the committee will say that, of all the systems of taxation examined by them, those in use in England, among the countries of Europe, and in Michigan and Wisconsin among the states of the Union, seem to them most intelligent, and in conformity with correct principles. The Michigan and Wisconsin systems would seem to be especially commendable. The systems in use in many of the older states, on the contrary, and nota-

bly in the states of Massachusetts, New York, Pennsylvania and
Ohio, are very cumbersome, and present hardly any features
worthy of study or imitation.

That of Massachusetts, for instance, is based upon no recognized principle, would admit of evasions in a most obvious way,
and is impossible of any general application. The fundamental
idea with it is, that the capital stock represents the property, and
that its market value will, therefore, approximately measure it for
purposes of taxation. A heavily bonded road, under this system,
practically escapes taxation ; and, again, where the stock is owned
outside of the state in which the road is situated, the tax levied
on it inures not to the state of the owner's residence but to that
in which the property is located. Under such a system it hardly
needs to be said that the taxation fluctuates widely in amount,
and that the amount of debt behind the capital stock being dis-
regarded, the burden bears little or no necessary relation to actual
earning capacity, whether net or gross. Clumsy and devoid of
scientific merit as it unquestionably is, however, the Massachusetts system would seem to be preferable to that still in use in
New York, concerning which the state assessors in their annual
report for 1873 expressed the opinion that under it there was " no
uniform rule for any road, in any county, each assessor being
governed entirely by his own views." In certain towns the railroads appear to pay about one-third of the entire taxes, while the
assessed valuation now (1878) varies from $400 per mile to $100
per rod.

"The difference in the assessment of the New York Central &
Hudson River Road, where, for all the purposes that the road
can be used, it is of the same value to the company, is $24,000
per mile. In short, it is scarcely an exaggeration to say that the
assessments are as unlike as the complexion, temperament and
disposition of the assessors." It does not need to be pointed out
that a system such as this — and it is the system in most general
use — compels the corporations, in self-defense, to an active par-
ticipation in local politics. Indeed, it is not too much to say,
that, as a system, it is open to almost every conceivable objection.

It does not seem necessary to proceed in the enumeration of
states, as the objections to which the system of each is open will

readily suggest themselves to any one at all familiar with the principles of correct taxation on reference to the accompanying abstract of these systems. It is very, very apparent that the subject of railroad taxation is one which in this country has as yet received very little mature consideration. With a view to affording some basis for better legislation, the committee submit with the accompanying documents the following form of law in which the phraseology of the Michigan statute has been very closely followed.

C. F. ADAMS, JR., of Massachusetts.
W. B. WILLIAMS, of Michigan.
J. H. OBERLY, of Illinois.
December 1, 1879.   *Committee.*

DRAFT OF LAW.

SEC. I. Every corporation, person or association owning or operating any railroad or any portion thereof in this state, shall on or before the —— day of —— in each year pay to the state treasurer an annual tax upon the gross receipts of said railroad, computed in the following manner, viz.: Upon all gross receipts not exceeding —— thousand dollars in amount per mile of road actually operated,—— per cent. of such gross earnings; upon such gross receipts in excess of —— thousand dollars per mile so operated, —— per cent. thereof, which shall be in lieu of all other taxes upon the property, capital stock or evidences of indebtedness of such corporations, except such real estate as lies outside of the location for a right of way exclusively, not exceeding — rods in width.

SEC. II. The real estate lying outside of such location, shall be liable to taxation in the same manner as other real estate in the same place.

SEC. III. When a railroad lies partly within and partly without this state, there shall be paid into the state treasury such proportion of the tax imposed by the first section of this act, as the length of its operated road in this state bears to the whole length thereof.

APPENDIX.

¹ Reports on the systems of railroad taxation in use in the following countries :

1. Austria.	6. Germany.
2. British America.	7. Holland.
3. Belgium.	8. Hungary.
4. England.	9. Russia.
5. France.	10. Switzerland.

AUSTRIA.

Legation of the United States,
VIENNA, _March_ 15, 1879.

SIR: In obedience to your instructions under date of Feb. 18, 1879, requesting information touching the system of taxation of railroads in this empire, I have now the honor to make the following report. The system of the two halves of the empire being established independently, as of two independent states, I give first that of Austria.

I. "On what general, recognized principle, if any, is the railroad taxation of Austria-Hungary based?"

A. On that of absolute assimilation to the system of taxation applied to individuals. The corporation is treated as if it were an individual owning the same property.

II. "In how far are the railroads taxed as owners of realty?"

A. All their realty is taxed. Their land, which is taken for the line from the adjoining agricultural lands, continues to be taxed as land at the same rate as the lands adjoining it. Their town real estate is taxed in the same manner as the neighboring private real estate is taxed. There is for all owners of realty a ground tax, distinguishing between the value of the land and of the buildings erected thereon. The same rule and rate apply to railroad real property in the town.

III. "In how far as holders of personalty?"

A. They are considered as having no personalty which is not either produced or represented by franchise or income, or net earnings of some sort. And all these are taxed on the same principle as those of individuals. In Austria all enterprises [_Erwerbe_, business undertakings] are taxed, whether undertaken by an individual, or a share company, from that of a shoemaker to that of construction of a great railroad. All are regarded in a certain sense as franchises and so are annually taxed, but usually to a very small amount.

IV. "In how far are they subject to a franchise tax?"

A. They are subject to no franchise tax differing in principle from that applied, as above stated, to individuals (*Erwerbsteuer*). The amount of the original concession, or franchise tax, in the case of share railroads is 15.75-100 florins, or about $7.55 per annum, a trifling amount of little significance, except as maintaining the principle of a franchise tax. But there is also by law an additional annual tax on the enterprise (*Erwerbsteuer*), regulated according to its capital and extent, and reaching at the highest 1,575 florins in the case of the largest enterprises, and as the *ordinary* tax.

V. "In how far is their stock taxed as personalty to its owners?"

A. Each share usually represents the nominal value of two hundred florins, with the exception (I believe of the *Nordbahn*), where they are issued at the rate of one thousand florins per share. The issue of shares and of provisional certificates is subject to a stamp duty of fl. 1.25-100 for each fl. 200 of nominal value. At the same rate is taxed the issue of priority bonds issued by the company to their purchasers; except that when the bonds are temporary, having less than ten years to run, and are issued in a particular name, the rate of tax is reduced to fl. 1.25-100 for each fl. 400 of nominal value; that is to say, is reduced one half.

When the bonds or shares bear coupons calling for twenty florins or less, each coupon bears a stamp-tax of seven Kreuzers (3½ cents). When the coupon calls for larger sums, their stamp duty amounts to about 3⅛ per mile. These stamp duties properly affect the owner of the coupon, but are in fact usually assumed and paid by the company.

There appears to be no annual tax upon shares, as such; but income from them is fully taxed to the owner, at the income rate fixed by law.

VI. "What taxes are levied on the receipts of the companies, whether net or gross?"

A. Net receipts are ascertained as follows : All collections of money for transport, whether of passengers, baggage, freight, express goods, or other transport charges, and all sums derived from the letting, or rent, or other usufruct, of property which is not subject to other taxation — as to the land and house tax, for example — constitutes the *gross* receipts. From this aggregate may be deducted the sums disbursed —

(*a*) for expenses of the administration of the company ;

(*b*) for current running expenses ;

(*c*) for maintenance of the road, including repairs, replacement of perishable property, of rails, bridges ;

(*d*) all stamps and taxes paid in the course of their business, and generally all expenses incurred in conducting their enterprise, and for maintaining an efficient condition of all its parts.

On the other hand, these may *not* be deducted from the gross income —

a) their payments of interest ;

(*b*) the annual quotas paid for the liquidation of the capital, or of the bonded debt of the enterprise, nor any requirement of capital ;

(*c*) the fees paid to the directors for their services ;

(*d*) the contributions made by the company to the pension fund for their employees.

The balance thus ascertained constitutes the net income of the enterprise. The average of these *net* sums for three years is taken as the net annual taxable income of the enterprise. From this the franchise taxes (*Erwerbsteuer*) are deducted. Upon the residue an income tax of five per cent. is fixed as the regular tax for the next tax period of three years.

The taxes above mentioned are the regular legal rates, the *ordinarium*. But in late years the necessities of the treasury have increased. The annual finance law now establishes the *additional* levy to be made on this property ; so that, in fact, the present taxes are the double of the ordinarium, on income and franchise ; that is to say, amount to 10 *per cent. on the net income*, and in the case of the higher franchise to 3,150 florins (*Erwerbsteuer*).

N. B. The foregoing system is applied to the established and prosperous roads. Exceptions are made by law in favor of young

and unprofitable enterprises, which are sometimes relieved from some of these burdens by special enactments.   *   *   *
*   *   *   I have, etc.,

JOHN A. KASSON.

BRITISH AMERICA.

ST. THOMAS, Ont., *March* 17, 1879.

C. F. Adams, Jr., Esq., Boston, Mass.:

SIR : In the first place, I beg leave to state that the taxation of railroads, railroad property, securities and personalty is at what might be called its minimum in Canada, and complaints of railway corporations of excessive taxation are of rare occurrence.

In every case where an over-assessment occurs, there is a municipal court of revision to which appeal may be made, and, if such appeal be overruled therein, application for relief may be made to the county court judge of the county in which the tax is levied, who is empowered to examine on oath all parties interested ; and after hearing evidence as to value, his decision as to the proper assessment shall be final.

The railway interests of the country are zealously protected by the legislature.

In reply to your questions, I shall answer them *seriatim.*

First Question.—"Upon what general recognized principle, if any, is the railway taxation of the state in question based ? "

Answer.—There are no definite rules relating to taxation, except those laid down in the *Assessment of Property Act of the Province of Ontario*, 32 *Victoria*, Chapter 36.   Section 7 of this act reads as follows :

" The real estate of all railway companies is to be considered as lands of residents, although the company may not have an office in the municipality, except in cases where a company ceases to exercise its corporate powers through insolvency or otherwise."

And section 33 reads :

" Every railway company shall annually transmit on or before the first day of February, to the clerk of every municipality in which any part of the roadway or other real property of the company is situated, a statement showing, *first*, the quantity of land occupied by the roadway, and the actual value thereof, according to the average value of land in the locality, as rated on the assessment roll of the previous year; *secondly*, the real property, other than the roadway, in actual use and occupation by the company, and its value ; and *thirdly*, the vacant land not in actual use by the company, and the value thereof, as if held for farming or gardening purposes ; and the clerk of the municipality shall communicate such statement to the assessor, who shall deliver at, or transmit by post, to any station or office of the company, a notice addressed to the company of the total amount at which he has assessed the *real property* of the company in his municipality or ward, showing the amount for each description of property mentioned in the above statement of the company."

Second Question.— " In how far are the corporations taxed as holders of realty ?"

Answer.— Real estate consists, under the act, of the right of way and other lands acquired by the corporation for station grounds, shops and borrow-pits, and any lands requisite for the use and convenience of the railway proper. These lands are taxed *pro rata* with those adjoining, both in town and country, the assessor basing his estimate of value on the land itself, irrespective of the improvements on adjoining property.

Superstructure, excepting buildings, is exempt from taxation ; as are also rolling stock, engines, machinery, rails, sleepers, etc., etc., etc.

I may here add, that it is provided by Act of Parliament that municipalities may, at their discretion, exempt railway property from taxation of every kind. This is accomplished by a simple resolution in the municipal council of the town or township in which the property in question is situated.

Third Question. — " In how far as holders of personalty ?"

Answer. — Personalty is not ratable.

Fourth Question. — " In how far are they subject to franchise tax ?"

Answer. — There is no franchise tax.

Fifth Question. — " In how far is their stock taxed as personalty to the owners thereof ?"

Answer. — Their stock is not taxed, being exempted by clause

17, section 9, Assessment Act of Ontario, 32 Victoria, Chapter 36, which reads as follows:

"*Exemptions.* — The stock held by any person in any railway company."

Sixth Question. — " What taxes are levied on the receipts of the company, whether gross or net?"

Answer. — No taxes are levied on the receipts of the company.

Seventh Question. — "Where and how is rolling stock taxed?"

Answer. — Rolling stock is not taxed.

Eighth Question. — " How are the local taxes levied?"

Answer. — Each municipality and school-section collects its own taxes. County and township rates and statutory road labor are payable to the collector or township clerk, according to convenience. If paid to the latter, he remits the county rates to the treasurer of the county.

Ninth Question. — "What process of appeal is provided in cases of excessive assessment?"

Answer. — Court of revision, composed of members of the municipal council, and a further appeal to the judge of the county court.

I have the honor to be, sir,

Very respectfully your obedient servant,

R. F. HARRIS,
Claim Agent Canada Southern Railway.

BELGIUM.

Legation of the United States,
BRUSSELS, *May* 7, 1879.

SIR: * * * Referring to your No. 31, asking for particulars of railroad taxation in Belgium. * * *

The minister now proceeds to answer in detail the questions propounded. 1st and 6th. " On what generally recognized principle, if any, is the taxation of the railroads in Belgium based ?" "What taxes are levied upon the receipts of the companies, whether net or gross? "

The first article of the law of the 21st of May, 1819, upon the license duty, sanctions the following principle: No one can practice for himself, or any one in another's name, without having a license. An industry, or trade or shop is not exempted by Article 3 of this law. The license is based upon the proportionate amount of profit which each industry may realize, taking into account its usefulness, more or less great.

The workers of railroads are not by name indicated in the law of license duties. However, they are taxed by assimilation with contractors for transports.

The minimum duty is six francs, the maximum is 425 francs, in principal. The state collects besides 20 additional centimes upon this duty. The provinces and the parishes are authorized to add also some additional centimes, of which the amount varies according to their budget necessities.

Such is the system of imposing the license duty on railroad workers, in so far as they are not constituted into joint stock companies or into companies with limited liability by shares.

But in Belgium, the grantee railroad companies, all having a joint stock form, are taxed exclusively upon the annual profits.

It is understood by profits the interest of capital employed, the dividends, and generally all amounts divided in any titles whatsoever, including those which are affected by the increase of the social capital, and the reserve fund.

The duty is two per cent. upon these profits, independently of twenty additional centimes.

No taxation is due, when the joint-stock company closes its balance with a loss.

Second Question.—"In how far are railroads taxed, as holders of realty?"

The land necessary for the construction of conceded railroads for a service of public usefulness being acquired in the name of the state, which is the proprietor, the companies are only usufructuaries until the expiration of their grants of railroads.

The surface of land occupied by the railroads, being assimilated to the highways, is exempt from land tax.

The buildings which are inherent to the works are also exonerated from taxation, to wit: the squares and stations, warehouses, workshops, guard-houses, and buildings used for lodgings for station-masters.

2

In short, the only landed property on which the land tax is exacted is the surplus land, etc., which remains the property of the
grantees outside of the railway.

Third Question.—" In how far as holders of personalty ? "

In Belgium there is, properly speaking, no tax upon personalty.
However, the assessed taxes include a tax upon the furniture of
habitations.

The law which rules this tax is applicable to railroad companies,
as to all private persons, excepting for the furniture of offices and
buildings which serve exclusively for the working.

Fourth Question.— " In how far are they subject to a franchise
tax ?"

Such a tax does not exist in Belgium.

Fifth Question.— " In how far is their stock taxed as personalty
to its owners ?"

The stock and bonds of railroad companies are not subject to
any such special tax, but these " titles " [securities] fall under the
general application of articles 1 and 2. No. 2 of the stamp law of
the 21st of March, 1839, is thus worded :

" The stamp duty upon stocks and bonds, and all other deeds
for unlimited periods, is payable after five years of their issue. It
is fixed for those of 500 francs and under at fr. 0.50, for those
above 1,000 francs to 2,000 francs at fr. 2.00, and so on at fr. 1.00
per 1,000 francs without fractions."

Article 10 of the law of the 24th of March, 1873, exempts the
registering of *shares* issued by companies *whose business is established in the Kingdom.* * * * * * *

Very respectfully,

Your obedient servant,

WM. CASSINO GOODLOVE.

GREAT BRITAIN.

INLAND REVENUE, SOMERSET HOUSE, W. C.

March 27, 1879.

May it please your Lordships :

We have the honor to return the papers referred to us by your
lordships on the 18th instant, wherein the minister of the United
States seeks information as to the taxation of railways in this

country ; and we beg to submit the following replies to the questions put, as we understand them:

1. The taxation of railroads in Great Britain appears to have
been based on the previous taxation of stage carriages, which had
been in existence from the year 1779. The railroad tax does not
extend to Ireland. When the tax was first imposed, in 1832, the
charge was one half penny per mile for every four passengers, the
proprietors being required to keep accounts and pay duty monthly.
The development of railway traveling soon rendered necessary
a simple mode of assessing the duty, and, in 1842, the charge
was made five per cent. on the gross receipts from all passengers.

In 1844 a concession was made on behalf of the poorer class
of travelers, and all fares not exceeding a penny per mile by
trains stopping at every station were allowed exemption from
duty.

The duty on stage carriages was repealed in 1869, but railroads
having now obtained a practical monopoly in conveying passengers, and the tax having become an important branch of revenue, it is still maintained.

2 and 3. Railways are only subject to the usual stamp duties
in dealing either with real or personal property.

4. A franchise tax is not known in this country.

5. Railroad stock or debentures bear no tax as such.

6. Railroad proprietors, like other trading persons or companies,
are liable to income tax on their net annual profits, and such tax
is paid before any dividend is paid.

We have, etc.,

C. J. HERRIES,
ALGERNON WEST,
W. S. NORTHCOTE.

To the Lords Commissioners of Her Majesty's Treasury.

FRANCE.

[*Translation.*]

PARIS, *August* 30, 1879.

GENERAL: In your letter of March 4 last, you requested detailed information in regard to the system of taxation applicable
to French railroads.

The three following notes from the different bureaus having this matter in charge contain the information called for in the questions submitted by you.

Accept the assurances, etc.,

(Signed)   WADDINGTON.

GENERAL NOYES, Envoy Extraordinary, etc.

BUREAU OF LANDS AND STAMPS.

So far as the Bureau of Land and Stamps are concerned, the railway companies are subject to the following imposts:

I. Railway concessions to private companies are subject simply to the regular registration duty, all the official tariffs containing a formal clause to that effect. The sale of a concession to a third party, however, is subject to the impost of 2 per cent. on all sales of personal property.

II. Deeds of conveyance of real estate necessary to the construction of railroads are examined for the stamp and registered without any charges whenever the land is taken directly from the government, or whenever, as is usually the case, it is taken for a private company under the law of May 3, 1861, for public uses.

The assignment or awards for construction or equipment approved for railroads not chartered and not operated are subject only to the regular fixed duty.

The similar assignments or awards in the case of chartered roads are subject to the ordinary imposts. They accordingly are charged 1 or 2 per cent. on their capital, as the case may be, depending on whether they are or are not conveyances of personal property; unless the case falls under the laws of June 11, 1859, permitting the provisional registration at a fixed charge of contracts of a purely commercial character.

III. As respects their operation, railways are likewise subject to the regular impost. Accordingly tickets and baggage slips are subject, like individual receipts, to the stamp duty of 10 centimes (two cents) where the sum paid exceeds 10 francs ($2).

* * * * * * * * * *

IV. The stock and bonds of railway companies are subject to the same imposts as those of other companies, to wit: A stamp duty which is fixed for stock certificates at 50 centimes (10 cents) or one franc (20 cents) according to the duration of the company's charter, and at one per cent. invariably in the case of bonds. This duty may be converted by legislation into an annual tax of one twentieth of one per cent.

The certificates of stock and the bonds are further subject to a transfer tax of 50 centimes (10 cents). or, in the case of certificates payable to bearer, a regular annual tax of 20 centimes (five cents).

Finally, the stock, bonds and notes of railway companies are charged with a tax of three per cent. on their dividends or interest paid on them.

V. * * *

VI. Railroads operated by the state, so far as imports are concerned, are subject to the same taxes and contributions of every description as private railways.

Bureau of Direct Taxation.

The first three questions alone affect the Bureau of Direct Taxation.

1st. "On what principle, if any, is the taxation of railroads based ? "

Railways are subject to severe direct taxes, and share in their degree in the public burdens, according to their estimated revenues, in conformity with the principle of proportions, which is the fundamental idea of direct taxation in France.

2d. "In what degree are the companies taxed as holders of real estate ? "

The companies are subject to the land tax — a tax imposed on unimproved real estate in proportion to the net revenue derived from it. The right of way is assessed on the same basis as the best arable land of the town in which it is situated. The stations, buildings, etc., are assessed on the same basis as other improved property in the same town.

The companies further pay a tax, similar in character to the legacy tax, of 0.25 per cent. on all real estate held by them, which is neither included in their right of way nor used in their business as common carriers.

The companies further pay the window and door taxes on all

'buildings occupied by themselves or their employes. * * *
3d. " What license tax do they pay ? "

Each company is assessed at a fixed charge of 240 francs ($48)
primarily, over and above a graduated tax of 24 francs ($4.80)
for each myriameter (6 miles), and a proportional duty estimated
on the basis of a twentieth of the local valuation of the dwell-
ings and offices and of a fortieth of the buildings of the company,
necessary to the regular operation of its road. Certain permitted
local taxation is additional to the above.

The state is subject to the same payments as private companies.

Bureau of Indirect Taxation.

The first and sixth questions above relate to the Bureau of Indirect Taxation.

The law of October 1, 1798, fixed in a general way an indirect
tax on all conveyances, whether by land or water, proportioned to
the fare paid by the traveler. The law of February 24, 1805, has
extended this tax to the land carriage of merchandise. These
laws, though established prior to the invention of railways, have
been construed as applicable to them. Later the railways have
been specially designated in the laws of 1855 and 1871.

Under the laws of 1798 and 1805, the indirect tax amounted to
10 centimes (two cents) for each traveler and the same amount for
the carriage of all merchandise. A law of 1799 added to this as
a war tax an additional tenth. The law of 1855 added a second
tenth, which increased the tax to 12 per cent. Finally the law of
1871 fixed a further tax of 10 per cent. on the fares of railway
and steamboat passengers, as well as on the charges for the carriage of baggage and express matter, by the same means of conveyance. Menwhile, this law does not affect any charge less than
fifty centimes.

The principle which has prevailed in establishing the taxes on
railways is that this tax ought not to affect the official tariff fares,
and the total thus forms the sum paid by the traveler. Of this
total the companies retain the regular tariff fare and pay over to
the government, whose agents for this purpose they become, the tax
they have collected on its account.

* * * * * * * * * *

To sum up, on a net receipt of 100 francs, collected by the railroad companies on their own account, and made up of fares of 50 centimes (10 cents) or more, the additional imposts on account of the government and the total sum taken from the public are as follows:

```
Net receipt from regular tariff fares.....................  100.00f. = $20.00
Old imposts (Laws 1798 and 1805):
  Principal.......................... 10.00f.
  Two-tenths ........................  2.00  =         12.00  =     2.40
Additional tax (Law 1871).....  ........ 11.20          11.20  =     2.24
                                       ──────         ──────
  Total tax................. ........ 23.20f. = $4.80

  Total sum paid by public....................... 123.20f. = $24.64
```

Where the fare is less than 50 centimes (10 cents), the additional tax fixed by the law of 1871 is not levied. The figures then stand as follows:

```
Net receipts from regular tariff fares not exceeding 50 cen-
  times ......................................................      100f.
Old taxes (Laws 1798 and 1805) { Principal .......... 10f } 12f.   12
                                { Tenths ............. 2  }
                                                                  ──────
  Total taxes................................. ... .... 12f.  or 112f.
taken from the public.
```

The tax actually collected by the Bureau of Indirect Taxation on carriage by railways amounts therefore to 23.5 per cent. of the net receipts, and to 18.83 per cent. of the gross receipts on fares of 50 centimes (10 cents) or more, and of 12 per cent. of the net receipts of 10.71 per cent. of the gross receipts for fares less than 50 centimes (10 cents).

The calculation is based not on the carrying capacity but on the actual receipts of the companies from passengers and merchandise carried. It is payable every ten days, and is ascertained at the expiration of each tenth day from an inspection of the companies' registers by a superior official of the treasury.

The above described tariffs are applicable to the great railroad companies which carry on an extended traffic. But the merely local roads, the service of which is confined to the interior of certain large cities or within narrow limits about these cities, have the power, if they find the proportional impost as above calculated too onerous, to demand the privilege conceded by a law of 1833, modified by a law of 1839, under which a fixed impost is substituted for the proportionate impost in certain prescribed cases.

Under this law the following taxes are prices on carriages of

1 to 2 seats...............................	50.00f.	= $10.00 per annum.
3 "	75.00	= 15.00 "
4 "	100.00	= 20.00 "
5 "	120.00	= 24.00 "
6 "	137.50	= 27.40 "
Above 6 cents, for each additional seat with less than 50 seats in all................... .	12.50	= 2.50 "
For each seat above 50 and less than 150 inclusive.........	6.25	= 1.25 "
For each seat above 150 seats...............	3.12½	= 0.625 "

The imposts thus fixed are collectible monthly in advance. A law of the 21st of March, 1871, imposed an extraordinary and temporary tax of 5 per cent. on the cost of carriage of all goods sent by regular freight trains. This tax has been deemed obstructive to industrial development and abandoned from the 1st of July, 1878.

It may be interesting to know the result of the indirect taxation of railways in France. They are given below for the years 1875, 1876, 1877, 1878:

	Indirect.	Direct.	Total.
1875	55,566,210	13,495,782	69,061,992 =$13,808,398
1876	57,902,008	13,994,242	71,896,250 = 14,379,230
1877	57,457,166	14,045,322	71,502,488 = 14,300,293
1878	67,143,357	14,065,643	81,209,000 = 16,241,800

During the four years in which it was in operation (March, 1874, to July, 1878), the 5 per cent. tax on transportation of merchandise in regular trains returned on the average from 23,000,000 to 24,000,000 francs, annually.

GERMANY.

BERLIN, *April* 28, 1879.

The undersigned has the honor to state, in reply to the respected note of Mr. H. Sidney Everett, *Charge d' Affaires* of the United States of America, that the taxation of railroads and railroad bonds has as yet not been uniformly regulated in Germany, but that, on the contrary, it varies in the different German states.

Since, of all the states in question, Prussia alone possesses private railroads of considerable extent, the undersigned, in trans-

mitting the desired information, thought proper to confine himself
to the regulations in force in Prussia.

A more detailed review of the above will be found in the
memorial inclosed and respectfully placed at the disposal of Mr.
Everett by the undersigned, who also takes this occasion, etc.

(Signed)   Von Bulow.

To the *Charge d' Affaires* of the United States of America,
H. Sidney Everett.

Memorial concerning the Taxation of Railroads in Southern Prussia.

I. *State Taxes.*— It was already prescribed by law of November
3, 1838, concerning railroad enterprises (§ 38), that railroads were
to pay a tax, the regulation of which was, however, reserved for
a later period.

The law at the same time provided " that railroad companies
should remain free from license taxes (Gerwerbesteuer)." § 38.

The introduction of the tax provided for, ensued through the
law of May 30, 1853, concerning the tax to be paid by railroads.
Pursuant to the same, railroads are required to pay to the state a
percentage of their annual net receipts.

On March 16, 1867, a law was passed concerning the taxation
of all railroads not owned by the state, or by home stock companies, the provisions of which are in union with those of May
30, 1853.

Railroad bonds are not taxed as such by the state, but are subject, like all other evidences of indebtedness, to a single stamp
tax, the proceeds of which flow into the treasury.

II. *Other than State Taxes.*— The question as to whether and
to what extent railroads and railroad bonds may be taxed by
municipalities, circuits and other communal associations, is not
settled in Prussia by any legislative provisions.

The answer to this question depends rather, as railroads belong
either to the state or to stock companies, upon the provisions
which obtain as regards communal taxation of the fisc ——
and of stock companies, which are different in different parts of
the country.

To the six questions contained in the esteemed note of the 3d ult., an answer applying uniformly to the whole state can only be given with reference to the following points :

In so far as the realty of railroads is subject to the state realty or buildings tax, which is not the case as regards the roadbeds, the same are required to pay the taxes on realty imposed on the municipal and other communal associations, in particular with additions to the state realty and buildings tax.

As, in Prussia, municipal and circuit taxes are nowhere levied in the form of a property tax, there is no distinct taxation of railroads as owners of personalty.

Railroads are only entitled to immunity from taxation as regards roadbeds in so far as it is a question of the levying of communal real estate taxes.

The stock belonging, as well as the dividends accruing, to holders are everywhere subject as their personalty to the income tax of municipalities, circuits, etc. The right of deduction is also not at present conceded to holders in those municipalities in which a railroad as such is subjected to an income tax.

The interest accruing to owners of railroad bonds is taxed as their personal property in the same manner as the dividends of stockholders. A tax upon the bonds as such is nowhere imposed.

Communal and district taxes are nowhere imposed on gross receipts. In cases in which income taxation is imposed on railroads at all, the net receipts alone are regarded as subject to taxation. The surplus of the annual revenue over and above the annual expenditure, is considered the net receipts ; as expenditures are regarded also the customary annual loss by use of buildings, utensils, etc.; further, the necessary addition to the renewal fund, as well as the amounts expended to pay interest on debts, and commissions to officers, and members of the supervision and ministerial councils ; but not the amounts added to the capital reserve fund, or used for improvements to or enlargements of buildings.

Such taxation of the net receipts of railroads, however, only takes place on the basis of the special provisions contained in the regulations of the respective city and rural communities, in the city communities of the provinces of East and West Prussia,

Brandenberg, Pommerania, Silesia, Saxony, Slevic, Holsatia, Westphalia and Rhineland, in the city of Frankfort-on-Main ; and as regards private railways, in the city communities of the province of Hanover, then in the rural communities of the provinces of Westphalia and Rhineland, and further on the basis of § 14 of the circuit regulations of December 13, 1872, as regards the private railroads in the circuits in the provinces East and West Prussia, Brandenberg, Pommerania, Silesia and Saxony.

As entitled to tax are regarded only those communities and circuits in which there is a station ; and not those communities through which the road merely lies.

The apportionment of the entire net receipts of the railroad among the individual communities and circuits entitled to tax is based on the proportion of the gross receipts of the individual stations (internal business) to the entire gross receipts.

HOLLAND.

[Translation of Memorandum from the office of Minister of Finance.]

There are no special taxes on railway works; the railway companies are subjected to the same rates as other companies, except that the grants for the right-of-way, and an act of 9th of April, 1875, regulating the operating of railways by private companies stipulate some immunities in favor of the realm, viz:

1. Transport of soldiers and munitions, including horses, for half pay.

2. Free passage to policemen traveling on duty.

3. Free passage to people traveling under direction of the public authority.

4. Free passage to the mail.

5. Free passage to custom-house officers traveling on duty.

6. Offices free of rental for custom-house officials, and sufficient space for the erection of government buildings, for the state telegraph.

Answers to the six queries:

1. As above stated, there are no special railway taxes.

2. The railway companies pay for the ground they hold, the same rate of tax on realty as was paid for it before said

ground became its property; for the buildings on the ground the same tax is paid as would be for other buildings of a similar kind.

3. There is no tax on personalty, except a tax named *personal rate*, which is raised according to six bases, viz.: the rental, the value of the buildings occupied, the number of doors and windows in the buildings, the number of chimneys, the market value of their furnishings, the number of domestics and horses.

To this tax railway companies are liable. Their warehouses, like the warehouses of other kinds of business, are exempt.

4. They are not subjected to a tax on their shares or capital. They pay a license fee to an amount of two per cent. of their dividends, all business being liable for a license tax; their employes pay the same as all other clerks in trade.

5. Their shares and bonds are, at their issue, and when passing to inheritors, subjected to the same stamp duties and taxes as all other shares and bonds.

6. There is no tax on their net or gross receipts.

HUNGARY.

Legation of the United States,
VIENNA, *March* 30, 1879.

SIR: Referring to my dispatch No. 174, giving the information respecting *Austrian* railroad taxation, as desired by your dispatch No. 87, I now submit the following report touching the system adopted by the government of *Hungary:*

I. "On what general, recognized principle, if any, is the railroad taxation of Hungary based?"

A. On the principle that the *transportation* should pay the taxes, these being levied upon the passengers, and owners of the property transported. The particulars appear in the analysis of the Hungarian law here appended. (Enclosed I.)

II. "In how far are the railroad companies taxed as holders of realty?"

A. All the realty is exempt from taxation.

III. "In how far as holders of personalty?"

A. The personalty is also exempt from taxation.

IV. "In how far are they subject to a franchise tax?"

A. There is no tax on the franchise.

V. "In how far is their stock taxed as personalty to its owners?"

A. The shares are not subject to taxation.

VI. "What taxes are levied on the receipts of the companies, whether gross or net?"

A. There is no tax upon either gross or net receipts in Hungary.

Explanati on

With one or two exceptions, in both Austria and Hungary, the plan was early adopted of providing for the ultimate acquisition of the railroads by the government. To this end the concessions were granted for 90 years, with the condition that at the end of that period the whole franchise and property, with an equipment equal to the original amount, should revert absolutely to the state. To save the builders and owners from loss, a system of amortisation was established, in pursuance of which a certain portion of the capital in shares and bonds was to be refunded in each year, by which the reimbursement would be completed in ninety years. In principle it is a sinking fund. In Hungary the government guarantees the amortisation fund, and an interest of five per cent. on capital and bonded debts, in silver; and if the net earnings are not sufficient, the deficiency is made good out of the national treasury — but to be refunded if subsequent net receipts are sufficient. In point of fact, in the aggregate there is each year a deficiency of several millions charged upon the State Treasury of Hungary. Under such circumstances it is evident that taxes upon the corporation would involve the paying in of money with one hand only to be paid back by the other.

Hence the state levies its revenue upon passengers and freighters as a surtax upon the regular tariff charges of the railroads, these latter being the agents to collect it, and to account to the government.

In effect it is a tax on the gross receipts, while in law it is a tax on private business.

This explanation, together with the summary of the legal provisions hereto appended, will fully answer the inquiries so far as they relate to Hungary.

Some further elucidation of the railroad system is reserved for a subsequent dispatch, when some expected documents shall have been received at the Legation, showing more completely the legal provisions for Austrian railroads.

I have the honor to be, sir,

Your most obedient servant,

JOHN A. KASSON.

RUSSIA.

Legation of the United States,　}
ST. PETERSBURG, Russia, *March* 20, 1879. }

To the Honorable W. M. Evarts, Secretary of State, Washington:

SIR: Referring to your dispatch No. 39, addressed to Mr. Stoughton, relative to methods of taxation as respects railroads and railroad securities in use in Russia, I have the honor to report:

1st. That the railroad companies are free from taxation as holders of property, real or personal.

2d. The stock is free from taxation to its owners.

3d. On the 1st day of January, 1879, the government levied a tax of 25 per cent. on all passenger tickets of the 1st class, 20 per cent. on 2d class and 15 per cent. on 3d class. With the above exception, there is no direct tax on the receipts of the companies, net or gross.

4th. The railroad companies of Russia are under the control and exercise of the government, and by their respective statutes subject to a general franchise tax.

But before the usual conditions of a franchise can be satisfactorily stated, an explanation must be given of the method followed to obtain it.

The founders of the company must, in accordance with the form instituted for that purpose in the empire, present to the minister of ways and communication an outline of the enterprise.

By direction of the minister, the matter is then intrusted to a board of engineers belonging to the ministry, with instructions to examine and report as to the feasibility of the project, and to prepare plans and estimates of construction. If, after examination, it be deemed beneficial to give effect to the enterprise, the plans and estimates are placed by the minister before the committee of ministers for their consideration and action, and, if approved, are submitted for the inspection of his majesty the emperor.

After the imperial sanction has been obtained for the organization of the company, the ministers of ways and communication and of finance elaborate the conditions of the concession and the statutes of the company.

The concession, with the statutes elaborated and recommended by the ministers of ways and communication and of finance, is submitted to the committee of ministers, and, if approved, is presented for the inspection and sanction of his majesty the emperor.

The concession usually defines:

1st. The name, object and extent of the undertaking.

2d. The duty of the founders of the company, including the amount of caution money to be deposited by the founders in a government depository, in order to guarantee the establishment of the company within a specified time.

The statutes of the companies are the laws to be observed by the companies, and are invariably, after the sanction of the emperor, printed and filed among the collection of laws for the empire.

The following appear to me to be the principal provisions of the statutes of the various companies:

1st. They fix the duration of the franchises, usually from seventy-five to eighty one years, at the expiration of which period the exclusive ownership of the entire line, with all the real estate and rolling stock of the company, is vested in the government without any payment therefor.

2d. They specify the amount of the capital of the company, which is usually one-third in shares and two thirds in bonds.

3d. They define the number and dimensions of the postal cars to be furnished by each company for the gratuitous transportation of post officials, mails, packages, etc., etc.

4th. They exact the gratuitous use by the government of the company's telegraph.

" 5th. They define the quantity of rails, rolling stock, bridges, etc., which must be bought in Russia.

. 6th. They determine the percentage of reduction, usually from 40 to 75 per cent of the tariff, by which soldiers under arms are to be transported.

. 7th. They determine the percentage of the net receipts to be paid to the reserve fund and as dividends to shareholders.

8th. They concede to the companies, free of cost, all government land, stone or other material within certain specified limits, and which may be required for the legitimate use of the company in the construction or improvement of their lines.

9th. They declare the property, shares and bonds of the companies exempt from taxation.

10th. They guarantee to the companies an annual net revenue of (5) five per cent on the share and bonded capital.

I am trustworthily informed that with the exception of three companies the government pays annually to the various companies from 1½ to 4 per cent. of this guarantee.

The companies are all under the control of the minister of ways and communication, who, among other things, determines the tariffs for passengers and freights.

It will be seen from the statements here presented that the government takes away from the founders, substantially, the control and exercise of the roads. The above answers are therefore as complete as circumstances will admit of their being made, and I trust they will be found satisfactory.

I have the honor to be, sir, your obedient servant,

W. H. EDWARDS.

SWITZERLAND.

Mr. Hammer to Mr. Fish,

BERNE, *March* 25, 1879.

In answer to the note of the Chargé d'Affaires of the United States of the 10th inst., the Federal Council has the honor to furnish him with the following information:

I. The Swiss Confederation does not impose direct taxes; consequently the railway companies pay no contribution to the federal treasury. On the other hand, the companies are bound as regards the Confederation, by virtue of Article 19 of the law of Dec. 23, 1872, concerning railways:

a. To carry free of charge the letters and parcels, concerning which the prerogative of the state has reserved the right of transportation to the postal administration.

For the other parcels (*de messagerie*) expressed, the postal administration pays to the railway company a compensation calculated on the basis of the general express tariff (*tarif général de grande vitesse*) by calculating the weight of the parcels for one month, and, also, taking into account the diminution of the (*prestations*) contributions occasioned the companies by such transportation. If the Confederation and the companies cannot agree, the Federal Tribunal decides. The conductor attached to this service is carried free.

b. To carry free of charge the postal cars as well as their employees, and the persons charged with the inspection.

c. To pay an annual tax of concession of fifty francs for each section of one kilometre in operation, when the revenue of the operating attains four per cent. after deducting the amount for loss by wear and tear, or that assigned to the reserve fund. In the event of this revenue, thus calculated, attaining five per cent., the tax of concession may be raised to fr. 100, and to fr. 200, if this revenue is six per cent. or over.

II. Moreover, the cantons have the right to tax the railway companies in conformity with their legislation respecting taxation. Nevertheless according to the circumstances, not only have certain companies obtained from the cantons a complete exemption from taxation, while other railway enterprises have been called on to pay contributions to the cantons or to the communes, but there exists such a variety of provisions that it is not possible to fix a general principle applicable to the collection of these taxes.

The Federal Council regrets that consequently it is impossible to reply categorically to the questions specially presented by the Chargé d'Affaires of the United States, and it avails itself of the occasion to renew to him the assurances of its high consideration.

In the name of the Federal Council,

| The President of the Confederation, | HAMMER. |
| The Chancellor of the Confederation, | SCHIESS. |

3

SUMMARY OF LAWS IN RELATION TO RAILROAD TAXATION IN
FORCE IN THE VARIOUS STATES OF THE UNION.

[The states are in alphabetical order.]

ALABAMA.

Returns are made to a state board of the whole length of track, and of the length in each county and town ; also of the value of the road and of all real estate used for operating it, and of the rolling stock. The board finds the value of each mile of road, and notifies the assessors of counties and towns of the amount assessable by them, depending on the number of miles in their limits. They add the value of other real estate and of tools and machinery, and assess on the aggregate as on the estate of an individual.

The value of real estate is to be assessed as if owned in fee simple, without any deductions for mortgages or other cause. And the value of the whole road is never to be estimated as less than a principal sum, which, at 8 per cent., would produce the net earnings, meaning thereby the 'gross earnings less the running expenses.

There is no tax on receipts and none on individual holders of stock. From the state board there is no appeal. The penalty for not making returns is double taxation, obtained by adding one hundred per cent. to the assessable value as found.

ARKANSAS.

The county clerks of the several counties through which a railroad runs are constituted a board to annually "ascertain the value of all personal property, moneys and credits of such company, and appraise the same at its true value in money."

They may require detailed statements under oath, and in ascertaining values, road-bed, stations and other realty necessary to the daily running operations of the road are to be estimated as personal property.

The value thus ascertained is then apportioned by this board among the several counties through which the road runs, so that "to each county, and to each city, incorporated village, township and district, or part thereof therein, shall be so apportioned as shall equalize the relative value of the real estate, structures and stationary personal property of such company therein in proportion to the whole value of the real estate, structures and stationary personal property of such railroad company in this state; and so that the rolling stock of such company shall be apportioned in the same proportion that the length of such road in said county bears to the entire length thereof in all said counties or county, and to each city, incorporated village, township and district, or any part thereof therein interested, the amount apportioned to each county; and it is hereby made the duty of the county clerk to apportion the amount so found for his county to the cities, incorporated villages, townships, districts or parts thereof."

Where only a part of a railroad is in Arkansas, its entire value is appraised and divided in the proportion the length of road in Arkansas bears to its entire length, and "the principal sum for the use of the" road in Arkansas is determined accordingly.

In case of an alleged overvaluation, an appeal lies to the Board of Railroad Commissioners, which is authorized to reduce the valuation.

Neither the securities of the corporations in the hands of the holders thereof nor their gross or net receipts are taxed.

The right to levy additional tax on realty is in litigation.

The fundamental principle is that of a property tax levied upon an arbitrary valuation and paid directly by the corporation.

CALIFORNIA.

In this state before the adoption of the new constitution (1870), only material and visible property was taxed, excluding all franchises, stocks, bonds, etc. It was also assessed at full cash value.

Railroad corporations were taxed as holders of realty on the land occupied as right of way, with the track and all structures thereon as a whole, at a certain sum per mile. On land not used as track, railroads were taxed, like other property holders, on "the cash value of real estate," and separately on the "cash value of improvements" thereon. The personal property was assessed wherever it was found, except the rolling stock, which was assessed in each county through which the road ran in proportion to the length of road in each county. As above stated, no tax was laid on franchise or receipts, or on the stock of individuals. The assessment of each county was sent to the board of super-visors, acting as a board of equalization, hearing complaints and making valuations conform to actual cash value. Thence it went through the county auditor to the state board of equalization, con-sisting of the governor and two other officials, who levied a suffi-cient rate to raise the amount directed by legislation.

Each county board having received the state rate, collected the state tax, and both fixed the county rate and collected it. Munic-ipal authorities assessed and collected taxes on property found within each town or city.

Under the new constitution the property to be taxed includes credits, bonds, stocks, dues and franchises. A state board of equalization and county boards are provided for. The state board is to assess the franchises, roadway, roadbed, rails and roll-ing stock of all railroads running through more than one county at their actual value, and apportion it to each county and munici-pality in proportion to the length of road therein.

All other property is assessed in the place in which it is situated.

COLORADO.

The state board finds the value of all property, real and per-sonal, used for railroad purposes, considering all the circumstances of the road; and transmits to the county board of assessment the amount assessable by them in proportion to the number of miles of main track in each county.

CONNECTICUT.

Railroad companies are assessed one per cent. on such propor-tion of their stock and debt at market value less cash assets as the length of the road in the state bears to the whole length thereof, deducting the amount of local taxes paid on land not used for railroad purposes. The amount of municipal railroad bonds, of which the avails have been used for the road, is included as part of the debt on which taxes are assessed.

This is paid to the state treasurer, and is in lieu of all taxes on the property or rights of the company.

Individuals are not taxed either on the stock or securities of the railroad company held by them. No taxes are levied on the rolling stock nor on the receipts. The only local taxation is on land not used for railroad purposes. The state tax of one (1) per cent. is assessed on the amount as returned by the railroads and as corrected by the state board of equalization, whose decision is final.

DELAWARE.

Railroad corporations are taxed on land just as other owners of land are taxed, unless exempt by charter. They are not taxed on personal property. Nor are they taxed on their franchise, unless by charter provisions. A yearly tax of $\frac{1}{2}$ of 1 per cent. is laid on the actual cash. value. A tax is laid of 10 per cent. on net income, and when the road extends to other states, both these taxes are laid in proportion to the length within Delaware to the whole length of the road.

There is also a tax of 10 cents on each passenger carried within the state. Such a tax, as applied to persons brought into the state, or carried through it, or out of it, has been held to be unconstitutional by the Supreme Court of Delaware and of the United States. The law remains on the statute book, and is apparently enforced as to passengers only carried within the state.

An annual tax was laid of $100 on each engine, $25 on each passenger car, and $10 on each freight car or truck *used* during the year by any railroad company incorporated by or doing business in the state. But the act was declared to be unconstitutional by Justice Strong, of the Supreme Court of the United States, and an appeal which was taken was not prosecuted.

The Philadelphia, Wilmington & Baltimore Railroad Company pays, by statute authority, a commutation of $13,000, in lieu of the 10-cent tax on passengers; and other roads are permitted to commute in like manner. All the taxes, except that on land, are state taxes laid on amount returned by the company to the state treasurer, or in case of failure to return, computed by him. The tax on land is laid by local officers, with an appeal to the levy court.

FLORIDA.

Each road returns to the state comptroller the length and value of the road, including the right of way and rolling stock. The comptroller apportions the amount to each mile, and informs the county officers, who add to their county's share the other property in said county, and levy a tax on the aggregate as on the property of an individual.

GEORGIA.

When there is no charter exemption confining taxation to one-half per cent. of net income, the railroad companies are taxed, like individuals, on the value of roadbed, track, stations, rolling stock and all other property, real and personal. The rate has been ½ per cent. No tax is laid on franchise or on stock in the hands of owners.

The question of charter exemption has long been in litigation ; and the state has made many attempts to evade the constitutional protection given to roads by these contracts.

County taxes are levied at a per cent. on the state tax ; and on the same valuation. In case of alleged excess in valuation, the parties select arbitrators, who agree on an umpire.

ILLINOIS.

Taxes are levied on railroad corporations as on other corporations, and on individuals according to the value of their property.

The right of way, all tracks, stations and improvements on the right of way, are assessed by the state board of equalization.

All other real estate is assessed as the land of individuals is. All personal property, except rolling stock, is assessed wherever it is found on May 1. If the value of the capital stock exceeds the value of the real and personal estate, the increase is assessed as capital stock. There is no franchise tax, and no tax on stock to the holders thereof, nor is there any tax on receipts. The value of rolling stock is fixed by the state board, and distributed for taxation among the counties and municipalities, in proportion to the length of road therein.

The value of right of way, after being assessed by the state board, is distributed in like manner, except that side and second tracks and buildings on the right of way are taxed where they are situated.

There is no appeal from the state board. But the valuation fixed by local assessors may be revised by the town, and then by the county board, whose decision is final.

INDIANA.

The law of taxation is the same as in Illinois, except in three particulars:

(1) The whole capital stock is liable by law to be valued by the state board, and distributed for taxation to the counties and towns in proportion to the length of road in each. But this is not done, and this part of the law is obsolete.

(2) Railroad stock in the hands of individuals is taxed to them, as other stocks are.

(3) There is no appeal from excessive valuation.

IOWA.

The general principle is equality of taxation for all property. Assessments are made on the value of the entire railroad at the estimated value of each mile, including in the estimate right of way, bridges, rolling stock, stations and all other property exclusively used for railroad purposes.

There is no franchise tax nor tax on receipts; and shares are taxed at their market value to the holders thereof.

KANSAS.

The general principle of taxation is assessment on all property at its value in money. "Railroad property" is assessed by a state board, who estimate the value of the real estate connected with the right of way, and used in the daily operation of the road, including rails, ties, "franchises" and buildings. To this is added all moneys, credits and profits, all rolling stock, owned or used by the company. And the taxable value as ascertained by this addition is apportioned among the counties and municipalities in proportion to the length of road therein.

Real estate, not included in the above description, i. e., real estate not used in the daily operation of the road, is taxed like the land of individuals, in the locality where it lies.

Railroads are not subject to a franchise tax, whatever the word " franchises " in the law quoted above may mean. Nor are they taxed on receipts, except as they swell the amount of money or profits on hand in March, when the valuation is made. Stock is not taxed to its holders. · Local taxes are levied by local authori- ties on " railroad property," as returned to them by the state board of assessors. State taxes are apportioned by the state board, and collected by the county treasurers. Real estate, not " railroad property," is assessed by the local authorities, with an appeal to the state board, whose decision is final. Payment of taxes may be made by semi-annual installments. This method of assess- ment is said to have increased the amount on which taxes are levied by three million dollars over the old method of local assessment.

LOUISIANA.

In this state, the capital of all corporations is taxed, and property "over the capital" and property held in trust for busi- ness purposes for non-residents. Otherwise, there is no special provision.

MAINE.

No recognized general principle seems to govern the railroad taxation of this state. Railroad corporations are taxed for real estate in each town just as individuals are taxed for town pur- poses, but the track is not deemed to be real estate. They are not taxed for personal property. They are subject to a franchise tax of one and a half per cent. on the value of the franchise. This value is found by ascertaining the market value of the stock of each road, and deducting the value of the property subject to local taxation. When roads extend beyond the state, the value is pro- portioned to the length of line within the state. This is done by the governor and council.

The state treasurer credits each town according to the shares held therein ; and the remainder is retained by the state.

Stock is not taxed to the owners thereof. No taxes are levied on receipts, nor on rolling stock.

Local taxes are laid by each town on real estate outside of the location, with an appeal to county commissioners in case of exces- sive valuation.

In case of overvaluation by the governor and council, there is no appeal.

MARYLAND.

In this state, all taxation of railroads for state purposes is on gross receipts. County and municipal taxes are laid on property, as the declaration of rights requires all taxes to be. Real estate is taxed for county and municipal purposes where it lies. Personal property is taxed where the home office is established, when the railroad company has not a capital divided into shares or has shares wholly or in part exempt from taxation. If there is no home office in the state their personalty is not taxed.

Holders of stock are taxed thereon ; but in computing the value thereof, the assessed value of the real estate is deducted from the whole value of the capital stock, which is computed by the state tax commission. And an allowance is made on each shareholder's stock in proportion to this amount. The corporation pays the tax for each stockholder, and charges him with the amount.

The tax on gross receipts is one-half of one per cent., paid directly to the state treasurer.* Rolling stock is taxed at the home office, if that is within the state. Otherwise it is not taxed.

The appeal tax-court, in Baltimore, and the county commissioners in the several counties, correct valuations, and, under direction of the state tax commission and attorney general, strike off such property as is not subject to taxation.

The law as above stated is modified in regard to some railroad companies by their charters, which are irrepealable except by consent.

MASSACHUSETTS.

The assessors of each place annually report to the tax commissioner the names of corporations, except banks, established or owning real estate therein, with an account of the real estate and machinery in said place, and its value and the amount at which it is assessed, and also the amount of taxes laid for the year in said place. Each corporation returns a list of stockholders, with the number of shares held by each, the amount of capital stock,

* Where a road lies partly in another state, it is taxed on gross receipts on the number of miles in the state, if the company returns the same; otherwise on such proportion of gross receipts as the number of miles within the state bears to its whole length.

the par value and market value thereof; and also the real estate structures and machinery. Railroad companies, in addition, return the whole length of their lines, and the length lying without the state. Guardians, executors, etc., also make returns.

The tax commissioner ascertains the market value of the shares on May 1, preceding, and this is the taxable value of the franchise. The rate is determined by an apportionment of the whole amount. to be raised by property taxes in the state during the year, as returned by the assessors upon the aggregate valuation of all the towns and cities for the preceding year. From the valuation for railroad companies is deducted (1) an amount proportionate to that portion of their length lying beyond the state limits, (2) the value of real estate and machinery located and subject to local taxation within the state. An appeal is given, if the tax commissioner estimates the value of real estate and machinery at a less amount than the assessors have done.

Taxes are paid by the railroad corporations to the state treasurer, who is nominally tax commissioner, and who, with the auditor and one member of the council, constitute a board of appeal for correction of all errors, and their decision is final. Stock is not taxed in the hands of the holders thereof; nor is there any franchise tax, except as above stated, nor any tax on receipts. The proportion of tax received corresponding with the amount of stock owned in each city or town is credited to that place.

Land to the width of five rods taken for the railroad, is exempt from taxation; and so are all buildings for railroad purposes erected on such strip of land.

MICHIGAN.

In lieu of all taxes, except those on real estate not used for railroad purposes, a tax is laid of (2) two per cent. on gross earnings not exceeding $2,000 per mile, and of (3) three per cent. on gross earnings exceeding that sum. There is, also, a tax of three per cent. on receipts from passengers carried in any palace or sleeping car, or any car for which an extra price is paid; and a tax of two per cent. on gross receipts derived from the leasing or hiring of cars by any " special," " fast," " colored," or other freight line.

Real estate not used for railroad purposes is subject to local

taxes where it lies. There is no tax on the personal property o
railroad companies, nor on franchise, nor on rolling stock. Nor
is stock taxed in the hands of its owners. There is no apportionment of tax among counties or municipalities, the whole amount
being paid to the state and devoted to special purposes.

The railroads incorporated before 1850 were subject to an
annual tax of ¾ of one per cent. on their capital stock and all
loans used in construction. The Lake Shore and the Michigan
Central are still taxed in this way.

MINNESOTA.

A tax of three (3) per cent. on gross earnings is laid in lieu of
all other taxes, but by special legislation the amount of tax has
been reduced for some roads for a term of years, including the
Northern Pacific.

Taxes for each year are assessed on the earnings for the year
preceding.

MISSISSIPPI.

A franchise tax of $80 per mile, and of $40 per mile for narrow-
gauge road, is laid, in full of all state, county and municipal
taxes on railroad property.

Real estate not used for railroad purposes is taxed locally, like
the land of individuals. And the same is true of personal property
not used for railroad purposes. Stock is taxed to its holder at its
market value. No tax is laid on receipts, nor on rolling stock.

One-half of the franchise tax goes to the counties through
which the road runs; the balance to the state. Towns are pro-
hibited from taxing the roads running through them. There is
no appeal, nor any occasion for it,

MISSOURI.

The constitution of Missouri provides that all railroad corporations in the state, or doing business therein, shall be subject to
taxation on all property owned or used by them, and on gross or
net earnings, and on franchises and capital stock.

The law provides that, for purposes of taxation, each road shall
furnish the state auditor a statement of the length of the road, and
of extra tracks, with depots, water-tanks and turn-tables; the
length in each county and municipality; the number of engines

and cars and all other movable property owned or used by them, and the value thereof. Like statements are sent to each county court.

The statement may be revised by said court, and all property omitted is taxed at double its cash value. The state board of assessment and equalization revises the estimates. When a road extends into another state, where rolling stock is taxed, such a proportion of the value of such stock as the length of the road in Missouri bears to the whole length thereof is taxed. ['Thus if a road was taxed on rolling stock in one other state, and extended into half a dozen other states where rolling stock was not taxed still the tax on such stock would only be proportionate to the whole length of the road.]

The state board apportions the value of the property above named to each county and municipality in proportion as the ratio of miles of each road therein to the whole length of the road in the state. And taxes are assessed on such apportionment.

Local taxes are assessed on all property not specified above, including lands, work-shops, round-houses and other buildings, furniture and other personal property, by local assessors in the county or municipality where such property is. The assessment is certified to the county court, with the rate of levy, and that court levies the tax on railroad property as on other estates, except the school tax. The average rate of this tax is ascertained by adding the local rates of all the school districts, and dividing the sum by the number of districts. Then taxes are levied on the railroad company on the proportionate value of said railroad property. [The distribution of the amount depends upon the fact whether counties and municipalities have subscribed to aid railroads, and also upon the number of children in each school district.] Lands and other property, not taxed under the general provisions for railroad property, are taxed in the school districts where they are situated.

No appeal lies from the decisions of the state board.

NEBRASKA.

Railroad officials list the road-bed, right of way, rolling-stock, fixtures and personal property, stating, also, the whole number of miles in the state and in each county.

This list is sent to the state auditor. The state board of equalization assess the property of a corporation at the cash value for each mile, and divides the whole amount by the number of miles, to get the value of each. In doing this, they use the report and any other information they can get. The board does not assess the value of any machine shop or any buildings or grounds or of any other real estate; but the assessors of "each city or ward or precinct" assess these. The auditor certifies to the county clerks in the counties where the railroad property lies, the amount per mile on the number of miles assessed, and the amount in each county. The county commissioners adjust the number of miles and amount among the various municipalities, adding 50 per cent. when a report has not been made by the railroad company.

There is no tax on receipts or on franchise.

NEVADA.

Railroad taxes are assessed on the cash value of the property in each county by the county assessors, both of real and personal estate. No franchise tax is laid, nor any tax on receipts; nor is stock taxed to the holders thereof. Rolling stock is taxed in each county in proportion to the length of road therein. Appeals lie to the county board of equalization.

NEW HAMPSHIRE.

Railroads are taxed on all their property, including road-bed, buildings, rolling stock and equipments, at the average rate of taxation in all the towns and cities of the state.

There is no tax on franchise, nor on receipts, nor is stock taxed to the holders thereof. The state board of equalization having found the value of the road, and assessed the tax thereon, divide one-fourth ($\frac{1}{4}$) of it among the towns through which the road passes, in proportion to the amount expended in each town for right of way and taxes. The other three-fourths is divided among the towns in proportion to the stock owned therein, and the state keeps the tax on shares owned by non-residents or persons unknown.

NEW JERSEY.

All railroad companies, unless exempt by charter, are taxed one-half per cent. on the true value of the road used by them, equipments and appendages. The company makes returns of this value; the railroad tax commissioners have power to revise it, and an appeal lies to a justice of the supreme court, who hears it summarily.

Upon all real estate owned or used for a road, except the main track 100 feet in width, railroad companies pay county and town taxes where it is situated, at one per cent. on the value, except that at the termini; each road may have ten acres with the buildings thereon, free from all county and municipal taxes.

The only special tax on personalty seems to be the state tax on "equipment and appendages;" and there is no other provision as to the rolling stock. There is no franchise tax, nor any on gross or net receipts. Stock is taxed in the hands of the owners thereof. Valuation for county and municipal purposes is made once in three years by the commissioner of railroad taxation. Personal property not connected with the road is taxed as it is to individuals.

Special provision is made, whereby the United New Jersey Railroad and Canal Company may pay a fixed sum, $298,128.96, in full of all state taxes on all its roads, on certain conditions.

NEW YORK.

In this state there are no taxes except local ones, and these are laid on the real and personal estate in each municipality according to its value, as taxes are laid on individuals. There is no franchise tax, nor any tax on receipts; nor is stock taxed to its holders.

And no special rule is followed as to the taxation of rolling stock. The valuation of the local assessors, if regularly made, is final.

OHIO.

All property is taxed on a basis of its true value in money. The real estate of each railroad in taxed in the place where it lies; but personal property is held to include the road-bed, water and wood stations, and all other such realty as is necessary for the daily running operation of the road. A board consisting of county auditors of the counties through which any railroad runs, estimates the value of all the personal property of the railroad ccmpany, including the above named items, and apportions it among the counties and municipalities through which it runs, so that to each "shall be apportioned such part thereof as shall equalize the relative value of the real estate, structures and stationary personal property of such railroad company" in the state, and so that the rolling stock (including that hired or run under control of the company) shall be apportioned to each county and place in proportion to its part of the whole road in the state. And when only part of the railroad is in the state, the principal sum to be apportioned is the proportion of the road in Ohio to the whole road. When the road is wholly in one county the auditor thereof acts as a board.

The county boards report to a state board of equalization, which has power to raise or reduce the valuation of each road, provided that the aggregate valuation cannot be reduced. No appeal is provided.

There is no franchise tax, tax nor on receipts; and stock in the hands of individuals is taxed to them.

OREGON.

The only provision peculiar to railroads seems to be that rolling stock is taxed in the county where the principal depot or business is done, but if either terminus or any depot is in the county where the principal office is, it shall be taxed there.

PENNSYLVANIA.

All railroad companies paying dividends of six per cent. or more, pay a state tax of one-half mill on each dollar of capital stock; when the dividend is less than six per cent., the tax is three mills upon each dollar of appraised value of capital stock.

In addition to this all railroad companies (and also telegraph, palace car and sleeping-car companies) pay a tax of $\frac{8}{10}$ per cent. on gross receipts. Rolling stock is not separately taxed. No tax is laid on franchises, and no tax is assessed on shares.

Railroads themselves and all real estate and structures essential for operating the roads are exempt; but real estate and structures only incidentally useful for the transaction of railroad business are taxable locally.

A special act makes the real estate of railroads in Philadelphia, except superstructure and water stations, liable to local taxes. A similar act is in force in Pittsburgh.

If state officers are dissatisfied with the valuation of capital, another appraisal may be made; and an appeal may be had to the court. Excessive appraisals for local taxation may be reviewed by county commissioners. And local acts give appeals, in various places, to local courts.

RHODE ISLAND.

Railroad corporations are taxed like other corporations and like individuals on the value of their estates. Each town taxes the roads running through it on the value of its tracks and other real estate, but not apparently on personal property. No franchise tax is levied. Holders of stock are taxed according to its value. There is no apportionment nor any occasion for it.

Appeals may be made from the judgment of the assessors to town councils, but this is rarely done, as public notice is given to each person to state to the assessors his property and its value.

SOUTH CAROLINA.

The constitution requires equal taxation of all property according to its value. By law, the road-bed, right of way and stations are regarded as personal property. An annual return is made of the length of tracks, main and side; the value of all buildings, stationary engines, implements, rolling-stock, moneys and credits; also of the value of the whole road and equipments in and out of the state, and the value of the part within the state. The return also states how much of the track and of each item of property is in each county and in each town. A state board finds the value of the road-bed, right of way, rolling-stock, moneys and credits, and apportions it to each mile of the main track in or out of South Carolina. This valuation per mile is multiplied by the number of miles in the state, and in each county and town, and the product is the taxable valuation therefor. To this is added for the state the value of all the real estate, fixtures, stationary engines, machinery and stationary property, and for each county and town the value of such property situated therein. And on this amount is assessed the rate provided by law for the three classes of taxes.

There is no tax on franchise or on receipts; nor is stock taxed
to the holder thereof. There is no appeal, unless it should be
sought by injunction from the courts.

TENNESSEE.

In this state, the whole value of each railroad is taxed by assessors chosen for that purpose, who take into view the worth of the
property, the gross and net earnings, with all other facts bearing
on the true value. Real and personal estate is of course included,
and rolling stock as part of the personalty. No franchise tax is
laid, nor any tax on receipts as such. Holders of stock are not
taxed therefor.

When the valuation of each road has been fixed, the state tax
is laid thereon as on other property ; and the amount is divided
for local taxation according to the number of miles in each county
and municipality. An appeal lies to the three chief executive
officers of the state, who can appoint another board of assessors ;
and their action is final.

Some railroad companies in this state are protected from taxation by charter exemption not yet expired ; and such exemption
has recently been held to be valid by the supreme court of Ten-
nessee.

TEXAS.

Real and personal property are taxed by each county and municipality on the valuation of such property lying therein. The
road-bed and rolling stock are taxed in such localities according
to the mileage therein. There is no tax on receipts or on franchise. The holders of stock are taxed thereon as on other personal
property. The companies make returns as to property and values; assessors have power to change the valuation, and an appeal
lies to a county board of equalization, whose decision seems to be
final. In practice, various portions of the road are assessed at
different values and withour reference to the value of the road as
a whole.

VERMONT.

Railroad companies are taxed on real and personal estate on the
same principle with individuals, except that the road-bed and real
estate used for railroad purposes are taxable in each town at their

4

valuation, not exceeding $2,000 per mile of main line, but such roads are exempt from taxation on their realty for five years from the time when each begins to run regularly into or through any town in the state; and after eight years, it is subject to the general laws of taxation. As owners of personalty, including rolling stock, railroads are liable to the general law ; but part of that law is, that debts may be off-set in reduction of personalty; and the result is, that railroad personalty is never taxed. There is no tax on franchise or receipts. Holders of stock are taxed therefor as for other property. As to the assessment of road-bed, no appeal is allowed. Appeals from assessments on other real estate are made to local boards.

VIRGINIA.

The constitution provides for equal taxation of all property according to its value, and gives power to tax incomes in excess of $600 per year. Each road reports the value of all its real estate, specifying road-bed, stations and shops, and of all its personal property, specifying rolling stock and equipment, and also specifying the value in each county. The amount of gross and net earnings is also reported, and the amount of interest and dividends paid, payable and declared, to residents and non-residents. The whole length and the length of the road within the state are given, and the earnings are apportioned. The company is made collector of taxes on dividends and interest paid by it.

A tax of ⅓ of 1 per cent. is laid on the real and personal property of each road, one-fifth of which is applied to the public schools. On the indebtedness of each company, in lieu of the property tax thereon, a tax of fifty cents on $100 of the market value of the bonds is paid out of the interest due on such indebtedness. And this ;tax is collected by the company on non-residents as well as on residents.

There is no franchise tax. Holders of stock pay taxes according to its market value. Counties and towns receive the report made by the companies through the state auditor, and levy taxes on real and personal estate at the same valuation that is used by the state.

In general, an appeal lies from the valuation of assessors to two voters appointed by the parties, whose award is final.

WEST VIRGINIA.

Each company reports all its property in the state and the proportionate value of rolling stock, depending on the number of miles in the state as compared with the whole length of the road. This proportionate value and the value of all personal property, money, credits and investments is added to the real estate and apportioned to each county in proportion to the amount of real estate and fixed property therein as a basis for assessment. But all property, real and personal, used for railroad purposes, and all real estate which the company is allowed to hold, is to be assessed at its actual value, without regard to cost.

The board of works directs the auditor to assess for state and for general free school purposes on this valuation, and for free school purposes in town and school districts through which the road runs.

County supervisors apportion the amount to each town and district through which the road runs, according to the value therein.

If the report is not filed, or is not satisfactory, a board of commissioners is appointed of one freeholder from each congressional district, who assess as best they can.

The provisions for collecting are complicated.

Real estate used for any purpose not immediately connected with the road, is taxed like the property of individuals. When the capital of railroad (or other) companies is taxed, the stockholders are not taxed thereon.

WISCONSIN.

A state license tax takes the place of all state and local taxes on all real and personal property used for railroad purposes, except special assessments for local improvements in town and villages.

The following is the text in full of the Wisconsin statute, which imposes in fact a tax on gross receipts:

"The annual license fees for the operation of such railroads shall be as follows:

"1. Four per centum of gross earnings of all railroads, except those operated on pile and pontoon, or pontoon bridges, whose gross earnings equal or exceed three thousand dollars per mile per annum of operated railroad.

"2. Five dollars per mile of operated railroad of all railroads whose gross earnings exceed one thousand five hundred dollars per mile per annum, and are less than three thousand dollars per mile per annum of operated road, and in addition two per centum of their gross earnings in excess of fifteen hundred dollars per mile per annum.

"3. Five dollars per mile of operated road by all companies whose gross earnings are less than fifteen hundred dollars per mile per annum.

"4. Two per centum of the gross earnings of all railroads which are operated upon pile or pontoon, or pontoon bridges, which gross earnings shall be returned as to such parts thereof as are within the state.

" One-half of such license fee shall be paid at the time the license so issues, and one-half on or before the tenth day of August in each year."

www.ingramcontent.com/pod-product-compliance
Lightning Source LLC
Chambersburg PA
CBHW021643270326
41931CB00008B/1143